THIS DATING JOURNAL
BELONGS TO

_____

_____

# Dedication

This Dating Journal is dedicated to all the people out there who want to remember their dates and document their findings in the process.

You are my inspiration for producing books and I'm honored to be a part of keeping all of your dating notes and records organized.

This journal notebook will help you record your details about your dates.

Thoughtfully put together with these sections to record in detail: Name & Date, Favorite Things About The Date, What We Did, Where Did We Go, How Much Did I Spend, Things We Talked About, and much more!

# How to Use this Book

The purpose of this book is to keep all of your Dating notes all in one place. It will help keep you organized.

This Dating Journal will allow you to accurately document every detail about your going on your dates. It's a great way to chart your course through finding the perfect date.

Here are examples of the prompts for you to fill in and write about your experience in this book:

1. Name Of Date, Contact Info
2. Day & Time
3. Favorite Things About The Date
4. What Did We Do
5. Where Did We Go
6. How Much Did I Spend
7. How Much Did My Date Spend
8. Things We Talked About
8. My Screw-Ups
9. My Date's Screw-Ups
10. Conversation Rating 1-10
11. Kissing?
12. Sex?
13. Overall Rating Of The Date
14. Ideas For The Next Date
15. My Intentions
16. Notes

# *My Date* with _____

D A T E : _____          T I M E : _____

## My Favorite Things About The Date

- ☐
- ☐
- ☐
- ☐
- ☐
- ☐

Email: _____

Phone: _____

Address: _____
_____

### What did we do?
_____
_____
_____

### Where Did we Go?
_____
_____
_____

### How Much Did I Spend?
_____
_____

## Things We Talked About
_____
_____
_____

## How Much Did my Date Spend?
_____
_____

## My Screw Ups
_____
_____

## My Date's Screw Ups
_____
_____

Conversation from 1-10          1   2   3   4   5   6   7   8   9   10

 KISSING?

## IF YES

○ Bad Kisser

○ Mediocre Kisser

○ Good Kisser

## NO ○

## SEX?

## IF YES, WHERE?

○ My Place

○ My Date's Place

○ Somewhere Else

## NO ○

# HOW WAS THE DATE?

○ Never Again

○ Awkward

○ I've Had Better

○ Nice

○ Off the Charts

○ Love at First Sight

Ideas For Next Date?

_____

_____

My Intentions

_____

_____

Notes

_____

_____

_____

# *My Date* with _____

DATE: _____          TIME: _____

### My Favorite Things About The Date

- [ ]
- [ ]
- [ ]
- [ ]
- [ ]
- [ ]

Email: _____

Phone: _____

Address: _____
_____

### What did we do?
_____
_____
_____

### Where Did we Go?
_____
_____
_____

### How Much Did I Spend?
_____
_____

### Things We Talked About
_____
_____
_____

### How Much Did my Date Spend?
_____
_____
_____

### My Screw Ups
_____
_____

### My Date's Screw Ups
_____
_____

Conversation from 1-10     1   2   3   4   5   6   7   8   9   10

## KISSING?

### IF YES
- ○ Bad Kisser
- ○ Mediocre Kisser
- ○ Good Kisser

NO ○

## SEX?

### IF YES, WHERE?
- ○ My Place
- ○ My Date's Place
- ○ Somewhere Else

NO ○

## HOW WAS THE DATE?

- ○ Never Again
- ○ Awkward
- ○ I've Had Better

- ○ Nice
- ○ Off the Charts
- ○ Love at First Sight

Ideas For Next Date?

_____

My Intentions

_____

Notes

_____

_____

_____

# My Date with _____

DATE: _____     TIME: _____

## My Favorite Things About The Date

- ☐
- ☐
- ☐
- ☐
- ☐
- ☐

Email: _____

Phone: _____

Address: _____
_____

### What did we do?
_____
_____
_____
_____

### Where Did we Go?
_____
_____
_____
_____

### How Much Did I Spend?
_____
_____

## Things We Talked About
_____
_____
_____

## How Much Did my Date Spend?
_____
_____

## My Screw Ups
_____
_____

## My Date's Screw Ups
_____
_____

Conversation from 1-10     1   2   3   4   5   6   7   8   9   10

 KISSING?

IF YES                                          NO ○

○ Bad Kisser

○ Mediocre Kisser

○ Good Kisser

SEX?

IF YES, WHERE?                                  NO ○

○ My Place

○ My Date's Place

○ Somewhere Else

## HOW WAS THE DATE?

○ Never Again                    ○ Nice

○ Awkward                        ○ Off the Charts

○ I've Had Better                ○ Love at First Sight

Ideas For Next Date?

_____

_____

My Intentions

_____

_____

Notes

_____

_____

_____

# My Date with _____

DATE: _____                TIME: _____

## My Favorite Things About The Date

☐

☐

☐

☐

☐

☐

Email: _____

Phone: _____

Address: _____
_____

### What did we do?
_____
_____
_____

### Where Did we Go?
_____
_____
_____

### How Much Did I Spend?
_____
_____

## Things We Talked About
_____
_____
_____

## How Much Did my Date Spend?
_____
_____

## My Screw Ups
_____
_____

## My Date's Screw Ups
_____
_____

Conversation from 1-10    1   2   3   4   5   6   7   8   9   10

## KISSING?

### IF YES
- ◯ Bad Kisser
- ◯ Mediocre Kisser
- ◯ Good Kisser

NO ◯

## SEX?

### IF YES, WHERE?
- ◯ My Place
- ◯ My Date's Place
- ◯ Somewhere Else

NO ◯

## HOW WAS THE DATE?

- ◯ Never Again
- ◯ Awkward
- ◯ I've Had Better

- ◯ Nice
- ◯ Off the Charts
- ◯ Love at First Sight

Ideas For Next Date?

My Intentions

Notes

# My Date with _____

DATE: _____    TIME: _____

## My Favorite Things About The Date

- [ ]
- [ ]
- [ ]
- [ ]
- [ ]
- [ ]

Email: _____

Phone: _____

Address: _____
_____

### What did we do?

_____
_____
_____

### Where Did we Go?

_____
_____
_____

### How Much Did I Spend?

_____
_____

## Things We Talked About

_____
_____
_____

## How Much Did my Date Spend?

_____
_____
_____

## My Screw Ups

_____
_____

## My Date's Screw Ups

_____
_____

Conversation from 1-10     1  2  3  4  5  6  7  8  9  10

## ▶—♡—◀ KISSING? ▶—♡—◀

### IF YES
○ Bad Kisser
○ Mediocre Kisser
○ Good Kisser

### NO ○

## ♡ SEX? ♡

### IF YES, WHERE?
○ My Place
○ My Date's Place
○ Somewhere Else

### NO ○

## HOW WAS THE DATE?

○ Never Again          ○ Nice
○ Awkward              ○ Off the Charts
○ I've Had Better       ○ Love at First Sight

▶—♡—◀

Ideas For Next Date?

_____

_____

My Intentions

_____

_____

Notes

_____

_____

_____

# My Date with _____

D A T E : _____    T I M E : _____

### My Favorite Things About The Date

☐

☐

☐

☐

☐

☐

Email: _____

Phone: _____

Address: _____

### What did we do?
_____
_____
_____

### Where Did we Go?
_____
_____
_____

### How Much Did I Spend?
_____
_____

### Things We Talked About
_____
_____
_____

### How Much Did my Date Spend?
_____
_____

### My Screw Ups
_____
_____

### My Date's Screw Ups
_____
_____

Conversation from 1-10    1  2  3  4  5  6  7  8  9  10

 KISSING?

## IF YES

○ Bad Kisser

○ Mediocre Kisser

○ Good Kisser

NO ○

## SEX?

## IF YES, WHERE?

○ My Place

○ My Date's Place

○ Somewhere Else

NO ○

## HOW WAS THE DATE?

○ Never Again

○ Awkward

○ I've Had Better

○ Nice

○ Off the Charts

○ Love at First Sight

Ideas For Next Date?

_____

_____

My Intentions

_____

Notes

_____

_____

# My Date with _____

DATE: _____          TIME: _____

## My Favorite Things About The Date

☐

☐

☐

☐

☐

☐

**Email:** _____

**Phone:** _____

**Address:** _____
_____

### What did we do?
_____
_____
_____

### Where Did we Go?
_____
_____
_____

### How Much Did I Spend?
_____
_____

## Things We Talked About
_____
_____
_____

## How Much Did my Date Spend?
_____
_____
_____

## My Screw Ups
_____
_____

## My Date's Screw Ups
_____
_____

Conversation from 1-10     1   2   3   4   5   6   7   8   9   10

 # KISSING?

## IF YES
- ◯ Bad Kisser
- ◯ Mediocre Kisser
- ◯ Good Kisser

NO ◯

 # SEX?

## IF YES, WHERE?
- ◯ My Place
- ◯ My Date's Place
- ◯ Somewhere Else

NO ◯

# HOW WAS THE DATE?

- ◯ Never Again
- ◯ Awkward
- ◯ I've Had Better

- ◯ Nice
- ◯ Off the Charts
- ◯ Love at First Sight

Ideas For Next Date?

_____

_____

My Intentions

_____

Notes

_____

_____

_____

# My Date with _____

DATE: _____          TIME: _____

## My Favorite Things About The Date

- ☐
- ☐
- ☐
- ☐
- ☐
- ☐

Email: _____

Phone: _____

Address: _____
_____

### What did we do?
_____
_____
_____

### Where Did we Go?
_____
_____
_____

### How Much Did I Spend?
_____
_____

## Things We Talked About
_____
_____
_____

### How Much Did my Date Spend?
_____
_____
_____

## My Screw Ups
_____
_____

## My Date's Screw Ups
_____
_____

Conversation from 1-10     1  2  3  4  5  6  7  8  9  10

## KISSING?

**IF YES**

○ Bad Kisser

○ Mediocre Kisser

○ Good Kisser

NO ○

## SEX?

**IF YES, WHERE?**

○ My Place

○ My Date's Place

○ Somewhere Else

NO ○

## HOW WAS THE DATE?

○ Never Again

○ Awkward

○ I've Had Better

○ Nice

○ Off the Charts

○ Love at First Sight

Ideas For Next Date?

_____

_____

My Intentions

_____

_____

Notes

_____

_____

_____

# My Date with _____

DATE: _____          TIME: _____

## My Favorite Things About The Date

- [ ]
- [ ]
- [ ]
- [ ]
- [ ]
- [ ]

Email: _____

Phone: _____

Address: _____
_____

### What did we do?
_____
_____
_____

### Where Did we Go?
_____
_____
_____

### How Much Did I Spend?
_____
_____

## Things We Talked About
_____
_____
_____

### How Much Did my Date Spend?
_____
_____
_____

## My Screw Ups
_____
_____

## My Date's Screw Ups
_____
_____

Conversation from 1-10     1   2   3   4   5   6   7   8   9   10

 # KISSING?

## IF YES

◯ Bad Kisser

◯ Mediocre Kisser

◯ Good Kisser

NO ◯

# SEX?

## IF YES, WHERE?

◯ My Place

◯ My Date's Place

◯ Somewhere Else

NO ◯

# HOW WAS THE DATE?

◯ Never Again

◯ Awkward

◯ I've Had Better

◯ Nice

◯ Off the Charts

◯ Love at First Sight

Ideas For Next Date?

_____

_____

My Intentions

_____

Notes

_____

_____

# My Date with _____

DATE: _____          TIME: _____

## My Favorite Things About The Date

- ☐
- ☐
- ☐
- ☐
- ☐
- ☐

Email: _____

Phone: _____

Address: _____

_____

### What did we do?

_____
_____
_____

### Where Did we Go?

_____
_____
_____

### How Much Did I Spend?

_____
_____

## Things We Talked About

_____
_____
_____

### How Much Did my Date Spend?

_____
_____

## My Screw Ups

_____
_____

## My Date's Screw Ups

_____
_____

Conversation from 1-10     1   2   3   4   5   6   7   8   9   10

 KISSING?

## IF YES
○ Bad Kisser
○ Mediocre Kisser
○ Good Kisser

NO ○

## SEX?

## IF YES, WHERE?
○ My Place
○ My Date's Place
○ Somewhere Else

NO ○

# HOW WAS THE DATE?

○ Never Again
○ Awkward
○ I've Had Better

○ Nice
○ Off the Charts
○ Love at First Sight

Ideas For Next Date?

_____

_____

My Intentions

_____

_____

Notes

_____

_____

_____

# My Date with _____

DATE: _____      TIME: _____

## My Favorite Things About The Date

☐

☐

☐

☐

☐

☐

Email: _____

Phone: _____

_____

Address: _____

_____

### What did we do?

_____

_____

_____

### Where Did we Go?

_____

_____

_____

### How Much Did I Spend?

_____

_____

## Things We Talked About

_____

_____

_____

### How Much Did my Date Spend?

_____

_____

## My Screw Ups

_____

_____

## My Date's Screw Ups

_____

_____

Conversation from 1-10      1  2  3  4  5  6  7  8  9  10

 **KISSING?**

## IF YES
○ Bad Kisser
○ Mediocre Kisser
○ Good Kisser

## NO ○

## SEX?

## IF YES, WHERE?
○ My Place
○ My Date's Place
○ Somewhere Else

## NO ○

# HOW WAS THE DATE?

○ Never Again
○ Awkward
○ I've Had Better

○ Nice
○ Off the Charts
○ Love at First Sight

Ideas For Next Date?

_____

_____

My Intentions

_____

_____

Notes

_____

_____

_____

# My Date with _____

DATE: _____          TIME: _____

## My Favorite Things About The Date

- ☐
- ☐
- ☐
- ☐
- ☐
- ☐

Email: _____

Phone: _____

Address: _____
_____

### What did we do?
_____
_____
_____

### Where Did we Go?
_____
_____
_____

### How Much Did I Spend?
_____
_____
_____

## Things We Talked About
_____
_____
_____

## How Much Did my Date Spend?
_____
_____
_____

## My Screw Ups
_____
_____

## My Date's Screw Ups
_____
_____

Conversation from 1-10     1   2   3   4   5   6   7   8   9   10

# KISSING?

## IF YES
- ◯ Bad Kisser
- ◯ Mediocre Kisser
- ◯ Good Kisser

NO ◯

# SEX?

## IF YES, WHERE?
- ◯ My Place
- ◯ My Date's Place
- ◯ Somewhere Else

NO ◯

# HOW WAS THE DATE?

- ◯ Never Again
- ◯ Awkward
- ◯ I've Had Better

- ◯ Nice
- ◯ Off the Charts
- ◯ Love at First Sight

Ideas For Next Date?

_____

_____

My Intentions

_____

Notes

_____

_____

# My Date with _____

DATE: _____     TIME: _____

## My Favorite Things About The Date

☐

☐

☐

☐

☐

☐

Email: _____

Phone: _____

Address: _____
_____

### What did we do?
_____
_____
_____

### Where Did we Go?
_____
_____
_____

### How Much Did I Spend?
_____
_____

## Things We Talked About
_____
_____
_____

## How Much Did my Date Spend?
_____
_____
_____

## My Screw Ups
_____
_____

## My Date's Screw Ups
_____
_____

Conversation from 1-10     1   2   3   4   5   6   7   8   9   10

## KISSING?

### IF YES
- ◯ Bad Kisser
- ◯ Mediocre Kisser
- ◯ Good Kisser

NO ◯

## SEX?

### IF YES, WHERE?
- ◯ My Place
- ◯ My Date's Place
- ◯ Somewhere Else

NO ◯

## HOW WAS THE DATE?

- ◯ Never Again
- ◯ Awkward
- ◯ I've Had Better

- ◯ Nice
- ◯ Off the Charts
- ◯ Love at First Sight

Ideas For Next Date?

_____
_____

My Intentions

_____
_____

Notes

_____
_____
_____

# My Date with _____

DATE: _____    TIME: _____

## My Favorite Things About The Date

- ☐
- ☐
- ☐
- ☐
- ☐
- ☐

Email: _____

Phone: _____

Address: _____
_____

### What did we do?
_____
_____
_____

### Where Did we Go?
_____
_____
_____
_____

### How Much Did I Spend?
_____
_____

## Things We Talked About
_____
_____
_____

## How Much Did my Date Spend?
_____
_____
_____

## My Screw Ups
_____
_____

## My Date's Screw Ups
_____
_____

Conversation from 1-10    1  2  3  4  5  6  7  8  9  10

## KISSING?

**IF YES**

◯ Bad Kisser

◯ Mediocre Kisser

◯ Good Kisser

NO ◯

## SEX?

**IF YES, WHERE?**

◯ My Place

◯ My Date's Place

◯ Somewhere Else

NO ◯

## HOW WAS THE DATE?

◯ Never Again

◯ Awkward

◯ I've Had Better

◯ Nice

◯ Off the Charts

◯ Love at First Sight

Ideas For Next Date?

My Intentions

Notes

# My Date with _____

DATE: _____    TIME: _____

## My Favorite Things About The Date

- [ ]
- [ ]
- [ ]
- [ ]
- [ ]
- [ ]

Email: _____

Phone: _____

_____

Address: _____

_____

### What did we do?

_____
_____
_____

### Where Did we Go?

_____
_____
_____

### How Much Did I Spend?

_____
_____

## Things We Talked About

_____
_____
_____

## How Much Did my Date Spend?

_____
_____

## My Screw Ups

_____
_____

## My Date's Screw Ups

_____
_____

Conversation from 1-10    1   2   3   4   5   6   7   8   9   10

## KISSING?

**IF YES**

○ Bad Kisser

○ Mediocre Kisser

○ Good Kisser

**NO** ○

## SEX?

**IF YES, WHERE?**

○ My Place

○ My Date's Place

○ Somewhere Else

**NO** ○

## HOW WAS THE DATE?

○ Never Again

○ Awkward

○ I've Had Better

○ Nice

○ Off the Charts

○ Love at First Sight

Ideas For Next Date?

_____

_____

My Intentions

_____

Notes

_____

_____

_____

# My Date with _____

DATE: _____      TIME: _____

### My Favorite Things About The Date

☐

☐

☐

☐

☐

☐

**Email:** _____

**Phone:** _____

**Address:** _____
_____

### What did we do?
_____
_____
_____

### Where Did we Go?
_____
_____
_____

### How Much Did I Spend?
_____
_____

### Things We Talked About
_____
_____
_____

### How Much Did my Date Spend?
_____
_____
_____

### My Screw Ups
_____
_____

### My Date's Screw Ups
_____
_____

Conversation from 1-10      1  2  3  4  5  6  7  8  9  10

## KISSING?

### IF YES
- ◯ Bad Kisser
- ◯ Mediocre Kisser
- ◯ Good Kisser

NO ◯

## SEX?

### IF YES, WHERE?
- ◯ My Place
- ◯ My Date's Place
- ◯ Somewhere Else

NO ◯

## HOW WAS THE DATE?

- ◯ Never Again
- ◯ Awkward
- ◯ I've Had Better

- ◯ Nice
- ◯ Off the Charts
- ◯ Love at First Sight

Ideas For Next Date?

My Intentions

Notes

# My Date with _____

DATE: _____          TIME: _____

### My Favorite Things About The Date

☐ _____

☐ _____

☐ _____

☐ _____

☐ _____

☐ _____

### Things We Talked About

_____
_____
_____

### My Screw Ups

_____
_____

### My Date's Screw Ups

_____
_____

Conversation from 1-10     1  2  3  4  5  6  7  8  9  10

Email: _____

Phone: _____

Address: _____
_____

### What did we do?

_____
_____
_____

### Where Did we Go?

_____
_____
_____

### How Much Did I Spend?

_____
_____

### How Much Did my Date Spend?

_____
_____

# KISSING?

## IF YES
- ◯ Bad Kisser
- ◯ Mediocre Kisser
- ◯ Good Kisser

NO ◯

# SEX?

## IF YES, WHERE?
- ◯ My Place
- ◯ My Date's Place
- ◯ Somewhere Else

NO ◯

# HOW WAS THE DATE?

- ◯ Never Again
- ◯ Awkward
- ◯ I've Had Better

- ◯ Nice
- ◯ Off the Charts
- ◯ Love at First Sight

Ideas For Next Date?

_____

My Intentions

_____

Notes

_____

_____

# My Date with _____

DATE: _____          TIME: _____

## My Favorite Things About The Date

☐ _____

☐ _____

☐ _____

☐ _____

☐ _____

☐ _____

Email: _____

Phone: _____

Address: _____

### What did we do?

_____

_____

_____

### Where Did we Go?

_____

_____

_____

### How Much Did I Spend?

_____

_____

## Things We Talked About

_____

_____

_____

## How Much Did my Date Spend?

_____

_____

## My Screw Ups

_____

_____

## My Date's Screw Ups

_____

_____

Conversation from 1-10          1  2  3  4  5  6  7  8  9  10

## KISSING?

**IF YES**

- ◯ Bad Kisser
- ◯ Mediocre Kisser
- ◯ Good Kisser

**NO** ◯

## SEX?

**IF YES, WHERE?**

- ◯ My Place
- ◯ My Date's Place
- ◯ Somewhere Else

**NO** ◯

## HOW WAS THE DATE?

- ◯ Never Again
- ◯ Awkward
- ◯ I've Had Better

- ◯ Nice
- ◯ Off the Charts
- ◯ Love at First Sight

Ideas For Next Date?

_____

_____

My Intentions

_____

_____

Notes

_____

_____

_____

# My Date with _____

DATE: _____          TIME: _____

## My Favorite Things About The Date

☐

☐

☐

☐

☐

☐

Email: _____

Phone: _____

Address: _____
_____

### What did we do?
_____
_____
_____

### Where Did we Go?
_____
_____
_____

### How Much Did I Spend?
_____
_____

## Things We Talked About
_____
_____
_____

## How Much Did my Date Spend?
_____
_____

## My Screw Ups
_____
_____

## My Date's Screw Ups
_____

Conversation from 1-10    1  2  3  4  5  6  7  8  9  10

## KISSING?

**IF YES**

- ◯ Bad Kisser
- ◯ Mediocre Kisser
- ◯ Good Kisser

NO ◯

## SEX?

**IF YES, WHERE?**

- ◯ My Place
- ◯ My Date's Place
- ◯ Somewhere Else

NO ◯

## HOW WAS THE DATE?

- ◯ Never Again
- ◯ Awkward
- ◯ I've Had Better

- ◯ Nice
- ◯ Off the Charts
- ◯ Love at First Sight

Ideas For Next Date?

_____

_____

My Intentions

_____

_____

Notes

_____

_____

_____

# My Date with _____

DATE: _____    TIME: _____

### My Favorite Things About The Date

- [ ] 
- [ ] 
- [ ] 
- [ ] 
- [ ] 
- [ ] 

Email: _____

Phone: _____

Address: _____
_____

#### What did we do?
_____
_____
_____

#### Where Did we Go?
_____
_____
_____

#### How Much Did I Spend?
_____
_____

### Things We Talked About
_____
_____
_____

### How Much Did my Date Spend?
_____
_____

### My Screw Ups
_____
_____

### My Date's Screw Ups
_____
_____

Conversation from 1-10    1  2  3  4  5  6  7  8  9  10

 # KISSING?

## IF YES                                    NO ◯
◯ Bad Kisser
◯ Mediocre Kisser
◯ Good Kisser

# SEX?

## IF YES, WHERE?                   NO ◯
◯ My Place
◯ My Date's Place
◯ Somewhere Else

# HOW WAS THE DATE?

◯ Never Again                ◯ Nice
◯ Awkward                    ◯ Off the Charts
◯ I've Had Better            ◯ Love at First Sight

Ideas For Next Date?

_____

_____

My Intentions

_____

_____

Notes

_____

_____

_____

# My Date with _____

DATE: _____          TIME: _____

## My Favorite Things About The Date

☐

☐

☐

☐

☐

☐

Email: _____

Phone: _____

_____

Address: _____

_____

### What did we do?
_____
_____
_____
_____

### Where Did we Go?
_____
_____
_____
_____

### How Much Did I Spend?
_____
_____

## Things We Talked About
_____
_____
_____

## How Much Did my Date Spend?
_____
_____

## My Screw Ups
_____
_____

## My Date's Screw Ups
_____
_____

Conversation from 1-10    1   2   3   4   5   6   7   8   9   10

## KISSING?

**IF YES**

○ Bad Kisser

○ Mediocre Kisser

○ Good Kisser

**NO** ○

## SEX?

**IF YES, WHERE?**

○ My Place

○ My Date's Place

○ Somewhere Else

**NO** ○

## HOW WAS THE DATE?

○ Never Again

○ Awkward

○ I've Had Better

○ Nice

○ Off the Charts

○ Love at First Sight

Ideas For Next Date?

_____

_____

My Intentions

_____

_____

Notes

_____

_____

_____

# My Date with _____

D A T E : _____     T I M E : _____

## My Favorite Things About The Date

☐ _____

☐ _____

☐ _____

☐ _____

☐ _____

☐ _____

Email: _____
Phone: _____

Address: _____
_____

### What did we do?
_____
_____
_____

### Where Did we Go?
_____
_____
_____

### How Much Did I Spend?
_____
_____
_____

## Things We Talked About
_____
_____
_____

## How Much Did my Date Spend?
_____
_____
_____

## My Screw Ups
_____
_____

## My Date's Screw Ups
_____
_____

Conversation from 1-10     1   2   3   4   5   6   7   8   9   10

## KISSING?

**IF YES**

NO ○

○ Bad Kisser

○ Mediocre Kisser

○ Good Kisser

## SEX?

**IF YES, WHERE?**

NO ○

○ My Place

○ My Date's Place

○ Somewhere Else

## HOW WAS THE DATE?

○ Never Again          ○ Nice

○ Awkward              ○ Off the Charts

○ I've Had Better       ○ Love at First Sight

Ideas For Next Date?

_____

_____

My Intentions

_____

Notes

_____

_____

# My Date with _____

DATE: _____     TIME: _____

## My Favorite Things About The Date

☐

☐

☐

☐

☐

☐

Email: _____

Phone: _____

Address: _____
_____

### What did we do?
_____
_____
_____

### Where Did we Go?
_____
_____
_____

### How Much Did I Spend?
_____
_____

## Things We Talked About
_____
_____
_____

## How Much Did my Date Spend?
_____
_____

## My Screw Ups
_____
_____

## My Date's Screw Ups
_____
_____

Conversation from 1-10     1  2  3  4  5  6  7  8  9  10

 # KISSING?

## IF YES
○ Bad Kisser

○ Mediocre Kisser

○ Good Kisser

## NO ○

# SEX?

## IF YES, WHERE?
○ My Place

○ My Date's Place

○ Somewhere Else

## NO ○

# HOW WAS THE DATE?

○ Never Again

○ Awkward

○ I've Had Better

○ Nice

○ Off the Charts

○ Love at First Sight

Ideas For Next Date?

_____

_____

My Intentions

_____

_____

Notes

_____

_____

_____

# My Date with _____

D A T E :                              T I M E :

## My Favorite Things About The Date

- [ ]
- [ ]
- [ ]
- [ ]
- [ ]
- [ ]

Email: _____

Phone: _____

_____

Address: _____

_____

### What did we do?

_____
_____
_____

### Where Did we Go?

_____
_____
_____

### How Much Did I Spend?

_____
_____

## Things We Talked About

_____
_____
_____

### How Much Did my Date Spend?

_____
_____

## My Screw Ups

_____
_____

## My Date's Screw Ups

_____
_____

Conversation from 1-10      1   2   3   4   5   6   7   8   9   10

 # KISSING?

## IF YES
- ◯ Bad Kisser
- ◯ Mediocre Kisser
- ◯ Good Kisser

NO ◯

 # SEX?

## IF YES, WHERE?
- ◯ My Place
- ◯ My Date's Place
- ◯ Somewhere Else

NO ◯

# HOW WAS THE DATE?

- ◯ Never Again
- ◯ Awkward
- ◯ I've Had Better

- ◯ Nice
- ◯ Off the Charts
- ◯ Love at First Sight

### Ideas For Next Date?

_____
_____

### My Intentions

_____
_____

### Notes

_____
_____
_____

# My Date with _____

DATE: _____ TIME: _____

## My Favorite Things About The Date

- ☐
- ☐
- ☐
- ☐
- ☐
- ☐

Email: _____

Phone: _____

Address: _____
_____

### What did we do?
_____
_____
_____
_____

### Where Did we Go?
_____
_____
_____

### How Much Did I Spend?
_____
_____

## Things We Talked About
_____
_____
_____

### How Much Did my Date Spend?
_____
_____
_____

## My Screw Ups
_____
_____

## My Date's Screw Ups
_____
_____

Conversation from 1-10    1   2   3   4   5   6   7   8   9   10

## KISSING?

**IF YES**
- ⃝ Bad Kisser
- ⃝ Mediocre Kisser
- ⃝ Good Kisser

NO ⃝

## SEX?

**IF YES, WHERE?**
- ⃝ My Place
- ⃝ My Date's Place
- ⃝ Somewhere Else

NO ⃝

## HOW WAS THE DATE?

- ⃝ Never Again
- ⃝ Awkward
- ⃝ I've Had Better

- ⃝ Nice
- ⃝ Off the Charts
- ⃝ Love at First Sight

Ideas For Next Date?

My Intentions

Notes

# My Date with _____

DATE: _____   TIME: _____

### My Favorite Things About The Date

☐

☐

☐

☐

☐

☐

**Email:** _____

**Phone:** _____

**Address:** _____
_____

#### What did we do?
_____
_____
_____

#### Where Did we Go?
_____
_____
_____

#### How Much Did I Spend?
_____
_____

### Things We Talked About
_____
_____
_____

#### How Much Did my Date Spend?
_____
_____

### My Screw Ups
_____
_____

### My Date's Screw Ups
_____
_____

Conversation from 1-10    1   2   3   4   5   6   7   8   9   10

# KISSING?

## IF YES
○ Bad Kisser
○ Mediocre Kisser
○ Good Kisser

NO ○

# SEX?

## IF YES, WHERE?
○ My Place
○ My Date's Place
○ Somewhere Else

NO ○

# HOW WAS THE DATE?

○ Never Again          ○ Nice
○ Awkward             ○ Off the Charts
○ I've Had Better      ○ Love at First Sight

Ideas For Next Date?

_____

_____

My Intentions

_____

_____

Notes

_____

_____

_____

_____

# My Date with _____

DATE: _____    TIME: _____

## My Favorite Things About The Date

- [ ]
- [ ]
- [ ]
- [ ]
- [ ]
- [ ]

Email: _____

Phone: _____

Address: _____
_____

### What did we do?
_____
_____
_____

### Where Did we Go?
_____
_____
_____
_____

### How Much Did I Spend?
_____
_____

## Things We Talked About
_____
_____
_____

## How Much Did my Date Spend?
_____
_____

## My Screw Ups
_____
_____

## My Date's Screw Ups
_____
_____

Conversation from 1-10    1  2  3  4  5  6  7  8  9  10

 KISSING?

## IF YES

○ Bad Kisser

○ Mediocre Kisser

○ Good Kisser

NO ○

## SEX?

## IF YES, WHERE?

○ My Place

○ My Date's Place

○ Somewhere Else

NO ○

## HOW WAS THE DATE?

○ Never Again          ○ Nice

○ Awkward             ○ Off the Charts

○ I've Had Better       ○ Love at First Sight

Ideas For Next Date?

_____

_____

My Intentions

_____

_____

Notes

_____

_____

_____

# My Date with _____

DATE: _____     TIME: _____

## My Favorite Things About The Date

☐

☐

☐

☐

☐

☐

Email: _____

Phone: _____
_____

Address: _____
_____

### What did we do?
_____
_____
_____

### Where Did we Go?
_____
_____
_____

### How Much Did I Spend?
_____
_____

## Things We Talked About
_____
_____
_____

## How Much Did my Date Spend?
_____
_____

## My Screw Ups
_____
_____

## My Date's Screw Ups
_____
_____

Conversation from 1-10    1   2   3   4   5   6   7   8   9   10

## KISSING?

### IF YES
- ○ Bad Kisser
- ○ Mediocre Kisser
- ○ Good Kisser

NO ○

## SEX?

### IF YES, WHERE?
- ○ My Place
- ○ My Date's Place
- ○ Somewhere Else

NO ○

## HOW WAS THE DATE?

- ○ Never Again
- ○ Awkward
- ○ I've Had Better

- ○ Nice
- ○ Off the Charts
- ○ Love at First Sight

Ideas For Next Date?

My Intentions

Notes

# My Date with _____

DATE: _____        TIME: _____

### My Favorite Things About The Date

☐
☐
☐
☐
☐
☐

Email: _____
Phone: _____

Address: _____
_____

#### What did we do?
_____
_____
_____

#### Where Did we Go?
_____
_____
_____

#### How Much Did I Spend?
_____
_____

### Things We Talked About
_____
_____
_____

### How Much Did my Date Spend?
_____
_____

### My Screw Ups
_____
_____

### My Date's Screw Ups
_____
_____

Conversation from 1-10     1  2  3  4  5  6  7  8  9  10

 KISSING?

## IF YES
- ◯ Bad Kisser
- ◯ Mediocre Kisser
- ◯ Good Kisser

NO ◯

## SEX?

## IF YES, WHERE?
- ◯ My Place
- ◯ My Date's Place
- ◯ Somewhere Else

NO ◯

# HOW WAS THE DATE?

- ◯ Never Again
- ◯ Awkward
- ◯ I've Had Better

- ◯ Nice
- ◯ Off the Charts
- ◯ Love at First Sight

Ideas For Next Date?

_____

_____

My Intentions

_____

_____

Notes

_____

_____

_____

# My Date with _____

DATE: _____          TIME: _____

## My Favorite Things About The Date

☐

☐

☐

☐

☐

☐

**Email:** _____

**Phone:** _____

**Address:** _____
_____

### What did we do?
_____
_____
_____

### Where Did we Go?
_____
_____
_____

### How Much Did I Spend?
_____
_____

## Things We Talked About
_____
_____
_____

## How Much Did my Date Spend?
_____
_____

## My Screw Ups
_____
_____

## My Date's Screw Ups
_____
_____

Conversation from 1-10     1   2   3   4   5   6   7   8   9   10

## KISSING?

**IF YES**

○ Bad Kisser

○ Mediocre Kisser

○ Good Kisser

NO ○

## SEX?

**IF YES, WHERE?**

○ My Place

○ My Date's Place

○ Somewhere Else

NO ○

## HOW WAS THE DATE?

○ Never Again

○ Awkward

○ I've Had Better

○ Nice

○ Off the Charts

○ Love at First Sight

Ideas For Next Date?

My Intentions

Notes

# My Date with _____

DATE: _____     TIME: _____

## My Favorite Things About The Date

- ☐
- ☐
- ☐
- ☐
- ☐
- ☐

Email: _____

Phone: _____

Address: _____
_____

### What did we do?
_____
_____
_____

### Where Did we Go?
_____
_____
_____

### How Much Did I Spend?
_____
_____

## Things We Talked About
_____
_____
_____

## How Much Did my Date Spend?
_____
_____
_____

## My Screw Ups
_____
_____

## My Date's Screw Ups
_____
_____

Conversation from 1-10     1  2  3  4  5  6  7  8  9  10

 KISSING?

## IF YES                                    NO ○

○ Bad Kisser

○ Mediocre Kisser

○ Good Kisser

⤐—♡—⤐ SEX? ⤐—♡—⤐

## IF YES, WHERE?                       NO ○

○ My Place

○ My Date's Place

○ Somewhere Else

# HOW WAS THE DATE?

○ Never Again                    ○ Nice

○ Awkward                         ○ Off the Charts

○ I've Had Better                 ○ Love at First Sight

Ideas For Next Date?

_____

_____

My Intentions

_____

Notes

_____

_____

_____

# My Date with _____

DATE: _____          TIME: _____

## My Favorite Things About The Date

- [ ] 
- [ ] 
- [ ] 
- [ ] 
- [ ] 
- [ ] 

Email: _____

Phone: _____

Address: _____

_____

### What did we do?

_____

_____

_____

### Where Did we Go?

_____

_____

_____

### How Much Did I Spend?

_____

_____

## Things We Talked About

_____

_____

_____

## How Much Did my Date Spend?

_____

_____

_____

## My Screw Ups

_____

_____

## My Date's Screw Ups

_____

_____

Conversation from 1-10     1  2  3  4  5  6  7  8  9  10

 KISSING?

## IF YES

NO ◯

◯ Bad Kisser

◯ Mediocre Kisser

◯ Good Kisser

 SEX?

## IF YES, WHERE?

NO ◯

◯ My Place

◯ My Date's Place

◯ Somewhere Else

## HOW WAS THE DATE?

◯ Never Again ◯ Nice

◯ Awkward ◯ Off the Charts

◯ I've Had Better ◯ Love at First Sight

Ideas For Next Date?

_____

_____

My Intentions

_____

_____

Notes

_____

_____

_____

# My Date with _____

DATE: _____          TIME: _____

## My Favorite Things About The Date

☐

☐

☐

☐

☐

☐

Email: _____

Phone: _____

_____

Address: _____

_____

### What did we do?

_____

_____

_____

### Where Did we Go?

_____

_____

_____

### How Much Did I Spend?

_____

_____

## Things We Talked About

_____

_____

_____

## How Much Did my Date Spend?

_____

_____

_____

## My Screw Ups

_____

_____

## My Date's Screw Ups

_____

_____

Conversation from 1-10     1   2   3   4   5   6   7   8   9   10

## ⟫———♡———⟪ KISSING? ⟫———♡———⟪

### IF YES
○ Bad Kisser
○ Mediocre Kisser
○ Good Kisser

### NO ○

## ⟫———♡———⟪ SEX? ⟫———♡———⟪

### IF YES, WHERE?
○ My Place
○ My Date's Place
○ Somewhere Else

### NO ○

## HOW WAS THE DATE?

○ Never Again        ○ Nice
○ Awkward            ○ Off the Charts
○ I've Had Better    ○ Love at First Sight

⟫———♡———⟪

Ideas For Next Date?

_____

_____

My Intentions

_____

_____

Notes

_____

_____

# My Date with _____

DATE: _____          TIME: _____

## My Favorite Things About The Date

- [ ]
- [ ]
- [ ]
- [ ]
- [ ]
- [ ]

Email: _____

Phone: _____

Address: _____
_____

### What did we do?
_____
_____
_____

### Where Did we Go?
_____
_____
_____

### How Much Did I Spend?
_____
_____

## Things We Talked About
_____
_____
_____

## How Much Did my Date Spend?
_____
_____

## My Screw Ups
_____
_____

## My Date's Screw Ups
_____
_____

Conversation from 1-10     1   2   3   4   5   6   7   8   9   10

## KISSING?

**IF YES**

○ Bad Kisser

○ Mediocre Kisser

○ Good Kisser

NO ○

## SEX?

**IF YES, WHERE?**

○ My Place

○ My Date's Place

○ Somewhere Else

NO ○

## HOW WAS THE DATE?

○ Never Again          ○ Nice

○ Awkward             ○ Off the Charts

○ I've Had Better      ○ Love at First Sight

Ideas For Next Date?

My Intentions

Notes

# My Date with _____

DATE: _____     TIME: _____

### My Favorite Things About The Date

- [ ]
- [ ]
- [ ]
- [ ]
- [ ]
- [ ]

Email: _____

Phone: _____

Address: _____
_____

#### What did we do?

_____
_____
_____

#### Where Did we Go?

_____
_____
_____

#### How Much Did I Spend?

_____
_____

### Things We Talked About

_____
_____
_____

### How Much Did my Date Spend?

_____
_____
_____

### My Screw Ups

_____
_____

### My Date's Screw Ups

_____
_____

Conversation from 1-10     1    2    3    4    5    6    7    8    9    10

## KISSING?

**IF YES**

○ Bad Kisser

○ Mediocre Kisser

○ Good Kisser

**NO** ○

## SEX?

**IF YES, WHERE?**

○ My Place

○ My Date's Place

○ Somewhere Else

**NO** ○

## HOW WAS THE DATE?

○ Never Again

○ Awkward

○ I've Had Better

○ Nice

○ Off the Charts

○ Love at First Sight

Ideas For Next Date?

My Intentions

Notes

# My Date with _____

DATE: _____    TIME: _____

## My Favorite Things About The Date

☐

☐

☐

☐

☐

☐

Email: _____

Phone: _____

_____

Address: _____

_____

### What did we do?

_____
_____
_____

### Where Did we Go?

_____
_____
_____

### How Much Did I Spend?

_____
_____

## Things We Talked About

_____
_____
_____

## How Much Did my Date Spend?

_____
_____

## My Screw Ups

_____
_____

## My Date's Screw Ups

_____
_____

Conversation from 1-10      1   2   3   4   5   6   7   8   9   10

# KISSING?

## IF YES
- ◯ Bad Kisser
- ◯ Mediocre Kisser
- ◯ Good Kisser

## NO ◯

# SEX?

## IF YES, WHERE?
- ◯ My Place
- ◯ My Date's Place
- ◯ Somewhere Else

## NO ◯

# HOW WAS THE DATE?

- ◯ Never Again
- ◯ Awkward
- ◯ I've Had Better

- ◯ Nice
- ◯ Off the Charts
- ◯ Love at First Sight

Ideas For Next Date?

_____

_____

My Intentions

_____

_____

Notes

_____

_____

_____

# My Date with _____

DATE: _____          TIME: _____

### My Favorite Things About The Date

☐

☐

☐

☐

☐

☐

Email: _____

Phone: _____

Address: _____
_____

#### What did we do?
_____
_____
_____

#### Where Did we Go?
_____
_____
_____

#### How Much Did I Spend?
_____
_____

### Things We Talked About
_____
_____
_____

### How Much Did my Date Spend?
_____
_____
_____

### My Screw Ups
_____
_____

### My Date's Screw Ups
_____
_____

Conversation from 1-10     1  2  3  4  5  6  7  8  9  10

# KISSING?

## IF YES
- ◯ Bad Kisser
- ◯ Mediocre Kisser
- ◯ Good Kisser

NO ◯

# SEX?

## IF YES, WHERE?
- ◯ My Place
- ◯ My Date's Place
- ◯ Somewhere Else

NO ◯

# HOW WAS THE DATE?

- ◯ Never Again
- ◯ Awkward
- ◯ I've Had Better

- ◯ Nice
- ◯ Off the Charts
- ◯ Love at First Sight

Ideas For Next Date?

_____

My Intentions

_____

Notes

_____

# My Date with _____

DATE: _____     TIME: _____

## My Favorite Things About The Date

- ☐
- ☐
- ☐
- ☐
- ☐
- ☐

Email: _____
Phone: _____

Address: _____
_____

### What did we do?
_____
_____
_____

### Where Did we Go?
_____
_____
_____

### How Much Did I Spend?
_____
_____

## Things We Talked About
_____
_____
_____

### How Much Did my Date Spend?
_____
_____

## My Screw Ups
_____
_____

## My Date's Screw Ups
_____
_____

Conversation from 1-10    1   2   3   4   5   6   7   8   9   10

## KISSING?

**IF YES**
- ◯ Bad Kisser
- ◯ Mediocre Kisser
- ◯ Good Kisser

**NO** ◯

## SEX?

**IF YES, WHERE?**
- ◯ My Place
- ◯ My Date's Place
- ◯ Somewhere Else

**NO** ◯

## HOW WAS THE DATE?

- ◯ Never Again
- ◯ Awkward
- ◯ I've Had Better

- ◯ Nice
- ◯ Off the Charts
- ◯ Love at First Sight

Ideas For Next Date?

My Intentions

Notes

# My Date with _____

DATE: _____          TIME: _____

## My Favorite Things About The Date

☐

☐

☐

☐

☐

☐

Email: _____

Phone: _____
_____

Address: _____
_____

### What did we do?
_____
_____
_____

### Where Did we Go?
_____
_____
_____

### How Much Did I Spend?
_____
_____

## Things We Talked About
_____
_____
_____

## How Much Did my Date Spend?
_____
_____
_____

## My Screw Ups
_____
_____

## My Date's Screw Ups
_____
_____

Conversation from 1-10     1   2   3   4   5   6   7   8   9   10

## KISSING?

### IF YES

◯ Bad Kisser

◯ Mediocre Kisser

◯ Good Kisser

NO ◯

## SEX?

### IF YES, WHERE?

◯ My Place

◯ My Date's Place

◯ Somewhere Else

NO ◯

## HOW WAS THE DATE?

◯ Never Again

◯ Awkward

◯ I've Had Better

◯ Nice

◯ Off the Charts

◯ Love at First Sight

Ideas For Next Date?

_____

_____

My Intentions

_____

_____

Notes

_____

_____

_____

# My Date with _____

DATE: _____  TIME: _____

## My Favorite Things About The Date

☐ 

☐ 

☐ 

☐ 

☐ 

☐ 

Email: _____

Phone: _____

Address: _____
_____

### What did we do?
_____
_____
_____

### Where Did we Go?
_____
_____
_____

### How Much Did I Spend?
_____
_____

## Things We Talked About
_____
_____
_____

## How Much Did my Date Spend?
_____
_____
_____

## My Screw Ups
_____
_____

## My Date's Screw Ups
_____
_____

Conversation from 1-10    1   2   3   4   5   6   7   8   9   10

## KISSING?

**IF YES**

- ◯ Bad Kisser
- ◯ Mediocre Kisser
- ◯ Good Kisser

**NO** ◯

## SEX?

**IF YES, WHERE?**

- ◯ My Place
- ◯ My Date's Place
- ◯ Somewhere Else

**NO** ◯

## HOW WAS THE DATE?

- ◯ Never Again
- ◯ Awkward
- ◯ I've Had Better

- ◯ Nice
- ◯ Off the Charts
- ◯ Love at First Sight

Ideas For Next Date?

_____

_____

My Intentions

_____

_____

Notes

_____

_____

_____

# *My Date* with _____

DATE: _____          TIME: _____

## My Favorite Things About The Date

- ☐
- ☐
- ☐
- ☐
- ☐
- ☐

Email: _____

Phone: _____

Address: _____
_____

### What did we do?
_____
_____
_____

### Where Did we Go?
_____
_____
_____
_____

### How Much Did I Spend?
_____
_____

## Things We Talked About
_____
_____
_____

### How Much Did my Date Spend?
_____
_____

## My Screw Ups
_____
_____

## My Date's Screw Ups
_____
_____

Conversation from 1-10      1  2  3  4  5  6  7  8  9  10

## KISSING?

**IF YES**

○ Bad Kisser

○ Mediocre Kisser

○ Good Kisser

NO ○

## SEX?

**IF YES, WHERE?**

○ My Place

○ My Date's Place

○ Somewhere Else

NO ○

## HOW WAS THE DATE?

○ Never Again

○ Awkward

○ I've Had Better

○ Nice

○ Off the Charts

○ Love at First Sight

Ideas For Next Date?

_____

_____

My Intentions

_____

_____

Notes

_____

_____

_____

# My Date with _____

D A T E : _____          T I M E : _____

## My Favorite Things About The Date

☐

☐

☐

☐

☐

☐

Email: _____

Phone: _____

_____

Address: _____

_____

### What did we do?

_____

_____

_____

### Where Did we Go?

_____

_____

_____

### How Much Did I Spend?

_____

_____

## Things We Talked About

_____

_____

_____

## How Much Did my Date Spend?

_____

_____

## My Screw Ups

_____

_____

## My Date's Screw Ups

_____

_____

Conversation from 1-10     1   2   3   4   5   6   7   8   9   10

## KISSING?

**IF YES**

$\bigcirc$ Bad Kisser

$\bigcirc$ Mediocre Kisser

$\bigcirc$ Good Kisser

NO $\bigcirc$

## SEX?

**IF YES, WHERE?**

$\bigcirc$ My Place

$\bigcirc$ My Date's Place

$\bigcirc$ Somewhere Else

NO $\bigcirc$

## HOW WAS THE DATE?

$\bigcirc$ Never Again

$\bigcirc$ Awkward

$\bigcirc$ I've Had Better

$\bigcirc$ Nice

$\bigcirc$ Off the Charts

$\bigcirc$ Love at First Sight

Ideas For Next Date?

_____

_____

My Intentions

_____

Notes

_____

_____

_____

# My Date with _____

D A T E : _____    T I M E : _____

## My Favorite Things About The Date

☐

☐

☐

☐

☐

☐

Email: _____

Phone: _____

Address: _____

### What did we do?
_____
_____
_____

### Where Did we Go?
_____
_____
_____

### How Much Did I Spend?
_____
_____

## Things We Talked About
_____
_____
_____

## How Much Did my Date Spend?
_____
_____

## My Screw Ups
_____
_____

## My Date's Screw Ups
_____
_____

Conversation from 1-10     1   2   3   4   5   6   7   8   9   10

 KISSING?

## IF YES

○ Bad Kisser

○ Mediocre Kisser

○ Good Kisser

NO ○

## SEX?

## IF YES, WHERE?

○ My Place

○ My Date's Place

○ Somewhere Else

NO ○

## HOW WAS THE DATE?

○ Never Again

○ Awkward

○ I've Had Better

○ Nice

○ Off the Charts

○ Love at First Sight

Ideas For Next Date?

_____

_____

My Intentions

_____

_____

Notes

_____

_____

_____

# My Date with _____

DATE: _____          TIME: _____

### My Favorite Things About The Date

- [ ]
- [ ]
- [ ]
- [ ]
- [ ]
- [ ]

Email: _____

Phone: _____

Address: _____
_____

### What did we do?

_____
_____
_____

### Where Did we Go?

_____
_____
_____
_____

### How Much Did I Spend?

_____
_____

### Things We Talked About

_____
_____
_____

### How Much Did my Date Spend?

_____
_____
_____

### My Screw Ups

_____
_____

### My Date's Screw Ups

_____
_____

Conversation from 1-10     1   2   3   4   5   6   7   8   9   10

 KISSING?

## IF YES

〇 Bad Kisser

〇 Mediocre Kisser

〇 Good Kisser

NO 〇

## SEX?

## IF YES, WHERE?

〇 My Place

〇 My Date's Place

〇 Somewhere Else

NO 〇

# HOW WAS THE DATE?

〇 Never Again

〇 Awkward

〇 I've Had Better

〇 Nice

〇 Off the Charts

〇 Love at First Sight

Ideas For Next Date?

_____

_____

My Intentions

_____

_____

Notes

_____

_____

_____

_____

# My Date with _____

DATE: _____          TIME: _____

## My Favorite Things About The Date

☐

☐

☐

☐

☐

☐

Email: _____
Phone: _____

Address: _____

### What did we do?
_____
_____
_____

### Where Did we Go?
_____
_____
_____

### How Much Did I Spend?
_____
_____

## Things We Talked About
_____
_____
_____

## How Much Did my Date Spend?
_____
_____

## My Screw Ups
_____
_____

## My Date's Screw Ups
_____
_____

Conversation from 1-10     1  2  3  4  5  6  7  8  9  10

## KISSING?

IF YES

○ Bad Kisser

○ Mediocre Kisser

○ Good Kisser

NO ○

## SEX?

IF YES, WHERE?

○ My Place

○ My Date's Place

○ Somewhere Else

NO ○

## HOW WAS THE DATE?

○ Never Again

○ Awkward

○ I've Had Better

○ Nice

○ Off the Charts

○ Love at First Sight

Ideas For Next Date?

_____

_____

My Intentions

_____

_____

Notes

_____

_____

_____

# My Date with _____

DATE: _____  TIME: _____

## My Favorite Things About The Date

- ☐
- ☐
- ☐
- ☐
- ☐
- ☐

Email: _____

Phone: _____

Address: _____
_____

### What did we do?
_____
_____
_____

### Where Did we Go?
_____
_____
_____
_____

### How Much Did I Spend?
_____
_____

## Things We Talked About
_____
_____
_____

### How Much Did my Date Spend?
_____
_____

## My Screw Ups
_____
_____

## My Date's Screw Ups
_____
_____

Conversation from 1-10    1  2  3  4  5  6  7  8  9  10

## KISSING?

**IF YES**

○ Bad Kisser

○ Mediocre Kisser

○ Good Kisser

**NO** ○

## SEX?

**IF YES, WHERE?**

○ My Place

○ My Date's Place

○ Somewhere Else

**NO** ○

## HOW WAS THE DATE?

○ Never Again

○ Awkward

○ I've Had Better

○ Nice

○ Off the Charts

○ Love at First Sight

Ideas For Next Date?

_____

_____

My Intentions

_____

_____

Notes

_____

_____

_____

# My Date with _____

### DATE: _____      TIME: _____

## My Favorite Things About The Date

☐

☐

☐

☐

☐

☐

Email: _____

Phone: _____

Address: _____

_____

### What did we do?

_____

_____

_____

### Where Did we Go?

_____

_____

_____

### How Much Did I Spend?

_____

_____

## Things We Talked About

_____

_____

_____

### How Much Did my Date Spend?

_____

_____

## My Screw Ups

_____

_____

## My Date's Screw Ups

_____

_____

Conversation from 1-10     1   2   3   4   5   6   7   8   9   10

## KISSING?

**IF YES**
- ◯ Bad Kisser
- ◯ Mediocre Kisser
- ◯ Good Kisser

NO ◯

## SEX?

**IF YES, WHERE?**
- ◯ My Place
- ◯ My Date's Place
- ◯ Somewhere Else

NO ◯

## HOW WAS THE DATE?

- ◯ Never Again
- ◯ Awkward
- ◯ I've Had Better

- ◯ Nice
- ◯ Off the Charts
- ◯ Love at First Sight

Ideas For Next Date?

_____

_____

My Intentions

_____

_____

Notes

_____

_____

_____

# My Date with _____

DATE: _____          TIME: _____

## My Favorite Things About The Date

☐ _____

☐ _____

☐ _____

☐ _____

☐ _____

☐ _____

Email: _____

Phone: _____

Address: _____

_____

### What did we do?

_____

_____

_____

### Where Did we Go?

_____

_____

_____

### How Much Did I Spend?

_____

_____

## Things We Talked About

_____

_____

_____

## How Much Did my Date Spend?

_____

_____

_____

## My Screw Ups

_____

## My Date's Screw Ups

_____

Conversation from 1-10          1  2  3  4  5  6  7  8  9  10

## KISSING?

### IF YES

○ Bad Kisser

○ Mediocre Kisser

○ Good Kisser

NO ○

## SEX?

### IF YES, WHERE?

○ My Place

○ My Date's Place

○ Somewhere Else

NO ○

## HOW WAS THE DATE?

○ Never Again

○ Awkward

○ I've Had Better

○ Nice

○ Off the Charts

○ Love at First Sight

Ideas For Next Date?

_____

_____

My Intentions

_____

Notes

_____

_____

_____

# My Date with _____

### DATE: _____       TIME: _____

## My Favorite Things About The Date

- [ ]
- [ ]
- [ ]
- [ ]
- [ ]
- [ ]

**Email:** _____

**Phone:** _____

**Address:** _____
_____

### What did we do?
_____
_____
_____

### Where Did we Go?
_____
_____
_____

### How Much Did I Spend?
_____
_____

## Things We Talked About
_____
_____
_____

## How Much Did my Date Spend?
_____
_____
_____

## My Screw Ups
_____
_____

## My Date's Screw Ups
_____
_____

Conversation from 1-10     1   2   3   4   5   6   7   8   9   10

 KISSING?

## IF YES

○ Bad Kisser

○ Mediocre Kisser

○ Good Kisser

NO ○

## SEX?

## IF YES, WHERE?

○ My Place

○ My Date's Place

○ Somewhere Else

NO ○

## HOW WAS THE DATE?

○ Never Again

○ Awkward

○ I've Had Better

○ Nice

○ Off the Charts

○ Love at First Sight

Ideas For Next Date?

_____

_____

My Intentions

_____

_____

Notes

_____

_____

_____

www.ingramcontent.com/pod-product-compliance
Lightning Source LLC
Chambersburg PA
CBHW051033030426
42336CB00015B/2851